Power-free Pantry

Bach Ly

Published by Bach Ly, 2024.

POWER-FREE PANTRY

First edition. March 5, 2024.

ISBN: 979-8230376378

Written by Bach Ly.

Table of Contents

Table of Contents

Dedicated to Kaikea Frame. Thanks for the inspiration.

Chapter 1 : Who keeps putting rotten food into my fridge?

• • • •

IN THE SWELTERING HEAT of Kalihi, cleaning out the vegetable crisper in the fridge was often my job. I remembered all the slimy heads of lettuces, oozing tomatoes, and dripping cucumbers that my mom worked hard to buy but did nothing to keep them from spoiling. The waste basket was ready to accept all those expired vegetables and I always thought to myself, "I'll never waste food like this."

Fast forward a few years to my own apartment, my own fridge, and my discovery that I have never learned how to cook; I was back in the kitchen staring at spoiling food I had poured my paycheck into. Stacks of half-eaten lunch plates crowded my counter, and I was carefully calculating how much money I was spending on takeout. Stunned at my numbers, I made a decision right there to learn how to cook. Nothing would save me more money than learning how to prepare my own meals.

If I had to go out to eat, I can't be food secure. My meals depend completely on if the restaurants are open or not. So the first step to food security was learning how to cook. I picked one recipe from a cookbook and practiced that dish until I could happily eat the final result. A common mistake I see new cooks make is not fully learning one recipe before they hop to the next one. Trust me, most of the time, it's not the recipe, it's most likely the way the cook prepared the food. Yet most people will blame the recipe and jump to another recipe where they'll continue to botch the process. After a few more recipe switches, they gave up on cooking but the recipes weren't the ones who made those ingredients taste bad. It was the cook. So this is my best advice to anyone who's learning the art of food preparation. Pick a dish that you could see yourself eating every day and practice that one dish until you like the way it comes out. Once you've mastered that one recipe, then you may move on to the next. That's how I went from eating my burnt lava curry to being able to whip up most dishes with a few ingredients. It wasn't easy, but the path to being a better cook is a simple one.

Food security became very important to me once my daughter was born. At the time, I was living off-grid on the Big Island, Hawaii. The land we were on is so far removed from the town that it takes us about an hour to reach Hilo. I wanted to be able to take care of my family's eating needs, so I developed this food storage system. I learned of a time when shipping to this island had stopped because of a broken boat harbor and the stores ran dry, leaving many people without access to fresh food after a major storm. Knowing that is possible made me so afraid that I knew I never wanted my family to suffer because we weren't prepared for something like that.

Due to the spotty nature of solar power in my rainy area, I had to figure out how to do this without power, so the most common method of freezing it and storing it in a chest freezer wasn't an option. So many of my suggestions will be made from this point of view. I know that there are still many homesteaders who struggle with electricity, so this book is for us. If you have power, this system will be more efficient because you have the extra option of freezing.

In this book, I'll be showing how one can store food for the long term so that if the stores were unavailable for months, their family will continue to eat well.

I don't want you to think that you have to store food because the world is ending; that's the last thing I want. Being food secure is such a wonderful feeling that I wish to share it with everyone. I have no idea what's going to happen next, but I know I have enough food to feed my family. That bit of security is enough to make me less fearful when I receive bad news like my partner lost his job or my own business isn't doing well.

In our food-rich society where the homeless are overweight, why is there not enough food education? Why are we never taught how to manage our food supply? Why is this brand new information to so many people? Having a refrigerator has been so easy that it's like all the food knowledge has disappeared from our generation.

But it doesn't have to be like that. Let us strive for this essential knowledge and let us take back the reins to our food supply together. Step one is to learn how to cook. I know this seems silly because what if you hate cooking?

Cooking is the ability to turn raw ingredients into food, and the food supply you're building is made of raw ingredients. If you wish to stock up on instant noodles, that's okay, but with prepared food of that nature, the number of dishes you can make from it is very limited. You can make one dish with many additions, but it'll always be instant noodles. When you learn how to cook, you can make many different dishes from one ingredient such as flour. With flour, you can make sandwiches, you can make tacos, you can make pancakes, you can make dumplings, you can make pizza, you can make gravy, you can make dinner rolls, and so on. You get it. So that's why I suggest you learn how to cook because your food supply will go so much further if you have the ability to use the ingredients in new ways.

As you read, you may think to yourself this is too much effort; why would anyone work so hard to make their food last longer? For these people, I ask them how many hours of your life do you trade to afford this food? How much effort are you willing to put in for a dollar raise? Yet once the food is in our care, we toss it in the icebox and forget about it. How many hours of work are you throwing away every week?

From this point on, I'll move forward with the belief that you know how to cook and are ready to take back control of your food supply.

Chapter 2: What do I eat again?

• • • •

OKAY, SO LET'S START with the basics. To know how to store food, we first have to learn what food we eat. Go grab five blank sheets of paper and a pen. Stop reading right now and go get it. No matter how great the information is, it does us no good unless applied. So I'm going to need you to do these tasks as they come up in the book, okay?

This is how I track my food intake from month to month. Yes, you called it. Grocery receipts are real time data printed just for you. Start digging into your pockets and purses! Ideally, we'll want to have about three month's worth of receipts. If you throw away your receipts, start collecting them right away. I assign a special spot in my purse for them so it's all in one place when I need it. If you don't have three months worth, start with a week's worth and work up to three months.

• • • •

TIME FOR THE CATEGORIZED Monthly list:

- Collect all the grocery receipts from the last three months.
- With a sheet of blank paper, write down these different categories with space to write your answers: Spices & seasoning, Grains, Canned food supply, Oil supply, Vegetables, Meats, Breads, Cooking ingredients, Snacks, Drinks, and Sweets.
- Looking over the receipts to write down each food item you brought under those categories.
- When you're done, write beside each item how often you buy it. Weekly or Monthly?

You can write it up by hand or use a basic template like the one below.

Food Items Inventory

Date

DATE	ITEM	CATEGORY	QTY	UNIT	COST PER UNIT	STATUS

https://bachgratitudeadventure.wordpress.com/

Now on a new piece of paper, draw a big line down the middle. On the top, write perishable on one side and write non-perishable on the other. Take a look at your monthly buy list and put each food item down on the new list in the right column.

• • • •

WHEN YOU'RE DONE, THE answer to all your food problems will become apparent.

• • • •

IF YOU'RE BUYING MORE perishable than you do non-perishable, you'll always have food to throw out because you can't eat as many perishables as you buy. It seems so simple yet this is the most common cause of domestic food waste. Why do we do this?

Because when we're shopping, we're imagining all the different meals we can do with that fresh food but we don't actually count how many meals we make per week or per month. We would rather have too much than not enough for our families, so we overbuy. When I first made my lists, I realized that 80% of my monthly food shopping was perishables while only 20% were non-perishable. I was buying the fresh meats, the fresh vegetables, the fresh bread, the fresh milk, and the fresh seafood. Now fresh food is amazing and having fresh ingredients is great.

When it comes to food storage, they're always the first to go bad.

You don't have to give them up, but you do have to increase the non-perishable side to gain food security. So I'm merely suggesting that you switch your buying focus onto the non-perishable side of your food supply for a while and the results will speak for themselves.

So now, we have two lists in front of us; A Categorized Monthly list of everything we buy and a perishable scale list. What is a good use for this information? If you don't have your lists yet, stop reading and go finish your lists. We will use them throughout the system so they're good to have on hand.

So now you know what you eat, how much you eat, and how often you buy those items. This is way more data than most people have ever gathered about themselves; be proud of getting this far.

• • • •

YOU'RE DOING IT, YOU'RE taking charge of your food supply.

• • • •

WITH THIS INFORMATION, we'll make a food plan for your next shopping trip. Half of the food war is fought in the kitchen, the other half is fought in the stores.

I want you to look at your Categorized Monthly list and look at the numbers. Let's assume you buy 3 packs of 8 bouillon cubes every two months. Now we're going to multiply those numbers so we get a good idea of how much you'll need for six months. 3 packs x 3 sets of months = 9 packs will last you 6 months. With this formula, we can figure out how much food it would take to last you 6 months.

What about the perishables?

You don't have to do this for the perishables because we know that they won't last for 6 months unless frozen. If you have a chest freezer set aside for food storage, then by all means, do this for perishables too. There is always the risk of losing your food storage with the loss of power in this case though so it's best to lean heavy on non-perishables even with a chest freezer backup. One of my favorite memories is when a power line fell down in front of my friend's home and effectively cut off his power for several days. Instead of crying over the melting chest freezers that he had packed, he held a three day feast where everyone helped him eat up his food supply. It was a fun but painful lesson nonetheless.

If you intend to can your perishables, you're way ahead of the game and will have the most secure method for an affordable non-perishable supply. But the amount of hours you'll put into learning and practicing the skill can be overwhelming if you're just starting off. Practice good food storage with your local groceries first until you're good enough to risk your own canned items. It's all a learning process and we're taking it one step at a time. Don't overload by focusing on the things that don't matter now. Right now, we're learning our eating habits and what we would need to have a food supply plan.

How to start a 6-month food plan

- On a new paper, title it a 6-month food plan
- Write down the different categories of food
- Transfer the non-perishable food items from your Monthly list to this new list.
- Calculate how much of each item you'll need to have a 6 months supply of the item.
- Write down the answer beside each item.

• • • •

WHAT'S ON THE MENU?

- Grab a new sheet of paper and title it Main Menu.
- Look deeply at your 6 months plan and see how many meals you can make from these alone.
- Write down all these meals under two groups of what needs fresh food and what can be made from non-perishables.

- Leave space for each ingredient that you need for each meal

How to use your menu is simple. When you realize something is spoiling in your food supply, look at your main menu and see what recipes you can use it in. This is handy when you have perishables. It also gives you a fair idea on what is currently in your supply and gives you a heads up to restock when you're running low on your basics.

With these four food reports before you, you now have an idea of what it would take for you to buy 6 months' worth of non-perishables that you consume and what meals you would make from this supply.

This will be the foundation of your food system.

Once you have a rock solid base of 6 months' supply, you can switch your focus back to fresh food but now you'll know how much you actually eat so you won't overbuy on these items and you'll feel secure whether or not the stores are open.

Now you have highly customized information about your very unique lifestyle. These papers are important and should be treated as such. May I suggest keeping them in a folder or better yet, on a clipboard in a safe dry spot. We wouldn't want to redo all this research every time we go shopping.

• • • •

YOU CAN'T CONTINUE in this book unless you finish making those five food reports about your situation and your current eating habits. So stop reading! Right now!

• • • •

FINISH THOSE REPORTS so the rest of the system will work for you. I hate sounding like a broken record, but knowledge is useless without the application of what you learned because you won't get the results you want from knowing. You get results from taking action with the knowledge you gained. I can know how great broccoli is for my body all day, but my body won't get the benefits of broccoli until I eat it. So don't mindlessly read this book and praise how useful this information is while doing none of the tasks and gaining zero benefits. I'd rather you do one task and never finish the book than to read the book and do none of the tasks.

Chapter 3: How do I store the food?

Now, with your handy dandy lists of food data, we're going to learn about each food item and the proper way to store those ingredients so that they'll last 6 months and longer.

• • • •

TIME TO MAKE YOUR "HOW to store food" list.

- With a new sheet of paper, write down "How to store and how long do they last" at the top of the paper.

- On this list, you will pull from your Categorized Monthly list each item.

- The two main questions you're asking in your research are what is the exact shelf life of this food item and how do I store it in ideal conditions.

- Whip out your phone or laptop and with your list beside you to guide the research, look up information on each item you eat.

- Don't look for the best before date because it's not the true expiration date. That date is merely a suggestion to when the product will taste the best, not a reference to when it spoils. Also, expiration dates are confused with the best before date so it's much better to ask for the exact shelf life of each item, and sometimes you'll find brand official times.

- The best prompt is this exact search term. "What is the shelf life of ________?" Fill in the blank with the items on your list.

- After you get the shelf life, use this search term. "Best ways to store ______" You're looking for what conditions they like to be stored in. Dry? Dark? Light sensitive?

- Once you get the answer, write it down on your How to store list next to the item.

- Repeat this process for each item but you don't have to do it all at once. Start with just a few items at first and continue adding to this list over time.

• • • •

The basic foods to always have on hand:

THERE ARE A HANDFUL of items that are always good to have on hand and they are oils, seasoning, and grains. Why? Because they are the base of most meals and if you have a good supply on hand, your family will continue to eat no matter what.

Let's start with oils and how long they can last. Different oils have different shelf lives, and you have to do research on the one you use to find out. When oil goes bad, they have an awful smell and taste making them unusable.

When you first buy your ingredient, with a permanent marker write the date on the containers.

This makes it easier to separate the older oil from the new and also gives you an idea of how long your oil can last in your current storing conditions. When it goes bad, you'll look at the date and know exactly how long it took for it to go bad. If your oil goes bad before the time your research has suggested, I would look into how you store it and if you looked up the right type of oil. Vegetable oil and coconut oil have very different storing needs and lifespans.

Olive oil is what I use, and it can last up to four years in ideal storage conditions. Oil is the backbone of most meals, and I use it in nearly all of my dishes from curry to stir fry to soups. So knowing that about myself, I took a look at my charts, and I saw that I buy a 3-liter bottle of olive oil every two months. So for me to have a year's supply of it, I would have to buy 6 liters of olive oil and store them well.

Olive oil likes to be kept dry, and I prefer the metal tins instead of the clear plastic bottles since olive oil doesn't like too much direct light. It's best left in a cool cupboard. This is the kind of information to keep on your "how to store food" list. By writing it all down on a single sheet, you can easily access the research without digging through your old tabs on your phone.

Next, we go to our spices and seasoning because we can't have a good meal without them, and they usually have long shelf lifespans. This is also where all your sauces and condiments belong such as mayo, ketchup, dressing, teriyaki, soy sauce, etc. Look honestly at your list of spices and realize that you don't use 80% of what you have on your shelf. You use a handful of spices consistently, and it is these spices that you should bulk up on. Sauces will have different shelf lives based on their brand sometimes, and picking the right amount of them to buy can be tricky. Some sauces have an amazing shelf life such as soy sauce, Worcestershire, and so on while others like ranch can go sour faster. Another interesting side note is that there are a lot of sauces that we keep in the fridge that don't belong there. So sauce storage is a thing to learn.

For the most part, spices keep well dry and cool in their containers for many months. Most of my spice supply can last a year or more in their ideal storage conditions. Most people buy spices on a whim and usually leave them on the shelf for years before they throw it out for being too old. It's better to have a limited spice shelf that you use daily than a vast collection that you don't use at all. I know it makes me feel like a fancy chef if I can brag about how many spices I have, and I've been on many spice kicks where I bought saffron to be fancy, but I end up never using it. So only invest in spices that you will use weekly if not daily.

Now we're at grains, which includes rice, beans, flour, wheat berries, processed grains like noodles, and so on. This is where we want to focus most of our buying power because it is a major player in most meals, and grains can last a very long time in the right conditions. Rice stored well can last for a year or more. Beans in their dried state can also last for years when kept well and in their canned state, they can last for two years. Wheat berries and other grains like buckwheat and barley can last years in dry and cool storage. Pasta noodles can last in storage for a year or more. Now these food items are the heart of our food supply system because at the end of the day, just having grains, oil, and spices will create a very basic meal but a meal nonetheless. So with these few items stored up to 6 months, we're free to avoid the stores for months on end if need be.

When you're using grains in the kitchen, I recommend putting them in clear containers on a visible shelf in your kitchen so that you can spot when trouble starts in any of them. That way, you can scoop out the moldy grains and watch out for a special grain pest. It's a small black beetle that resembles a stag horn beetle but it's much smaller. This little guy doesn't bite and doesn't make the food taste bad but he is still your stored grains' worst enemies. There have been a couple of times when I cooked him right into my rice before noticing him. You can pick him out and still eat the rice since he doesn't have a taste. My first experience with this little critter was finding him and his kids in a bag of rice that I had stored away for a couple of months. He loves rice, wheat berries, pasta noodles, and more. What will happen is that he will turn your grains into a fine powder after he poops it out. A good sign that he's there is that dust or powder will start leaking out of your bags when you move them. Sometimes their eggs are in store-bought grains, and once they hatch, they will multiply like bunnies. So you can help by dusting Diatomaceous earth into your grains to kill them off. Diatomaceous earth, also known as diatomite, celite, or kieselguhr, is a naturally occurring, soft, siliceous sedimentary rock that can be crumbled into a fine white to off-white powder. Please use food-grade Diatomaceous earth for this use. It will also help keep the grains dry and doesn't affect the food.

Fumigation of Grains

IN DRY CLIMATES, CLEANED grains need not be fumigated. However, since I live in a wet hot place, it's a practice that is very helpful against insect eggs. Half a pound of dry ice will be enough for 100 lbs. of grain. Place 1-2 inches of grain in a container, place the dry ice in, and then pour the rest of the grain on top. Place a lid on it loosely so that the dry ice smoke can escape, and then after an hour, seal the container tightly. If you try to seal it before the hour, the build-up inside the container will explode. Once you're done, make sure you have an airtight seal or this fumigation will not be effective. Why should you do this? Well, this will help keep insects out of your grains and 100 lbs. is a lot to waste. Another way to destroy insects in the grains is to heat a small portion of your grains at 150 degrees for about 20 minutes in your oven. Keep the oven door slightly open so that the temperature stays low. As long as the temperature does not go over 150 degrees, the grains will not be damaged. You can do this in a shallow pan, but you want something with sides to prevent grain loss. Allow the grains to completely cool before you place them in a clean container. You don't have to do this, but it will prevent food loss due to pests.

I store my rice in a 5-gallon bucket with the lid on. I've been told of rats chewing through the buckets before, but I have yet to see it in my own experience. I have to go check on it since I can't see at a glance if the rice has been invaded, but with fumigation, I don't have to. Rice stored like this can last for years. Some people put in DE while others use different herbs like bay leaves to keep pests away. Do your research and test your add-ons in small batches in case they affect the rice in ways you don't like before you throw them into your main storage.

Wheat berries are the grains used to make flour, and they can last very well for years in proper storage. Wheat berries can be milled into flour, and this flour will have its full nutritional value. It's a lot of hard work and expensive tools but in the long run, this process is better for storing flour since flour will lose most of its nutrition within a month of being milled. Wheat berries can be used in place of rice and cooked like such. It has a mild nutty flavor and is very fun to experiment with. A simple recipe for wheat berries is to make a simple chicken noodle soup and replace the noodles with wheat berries. Cook until they're soft and have taken on the flavor of the soup. Now it's like wild rice chicken soup.

Dried beans will last for years if kept dry and clean. They do not need to be fumigated, but they want to be stored in an airtight container. When you buy them, you can repack them in glass jars or well-sealing containers. They do require a long soaking time plus a long cooking time if you want to use them in meals. I try to plan my bean dishes in advance so that I can soak them overnight and have them ready to go in the morning. Since I don't always have this foresight, I often use canned beans since they're precooked and can go right into the pot when the idea crosses my mind. Both last for years and both are delicious. I store mung beans because they cook well, and I can also sprout them to have bean sprouts on hand for different recipes.

Let's talk about non-perishables.

NEXT, WE LOOK AT OUR canned foods. Yes, I want fresh vegetables for my family, and I'm not a fan of the lining they use in some cans, but if done well, your canned food supply will work in harmony with your grains so that you can have a variety of dishes long after you're done shopping. Again, I look at my lists and see that I buy 1 box of 12 cans of green beans per month. So for a year's supply, I would buy 12 boxes and I would not have to buy green beans again until next year.

Can you see where I'm going with this? Is the bigger picture becoming clear? From your 6-month food plan, you're learning how to start and maintain a year's supply of food for your family. Once you have the main food groups covered in non-perishables, you'll be able to buy the right amount of fresh and raw foods for your needs.

The two food items that will last the longest are grains and canned food.

The shelf life of cans can range from 12 months to 96 months plus. Colored fruit and other sweet items will have a shorter shelf life because of the natural fruit sugar in them. They can usually last about a year while other foods are storable for 3 years, and others will last for 8 years. According to my research, 2 percent to 5 percent of food nutritional value is lost each year, so it's a matter of time before all value is lost. So while it can last that long, with proper rotation, you would have eaten the food way before 8 years had passed, but it's nice to know that it can last that long.

The best way to store your cans is in a cool dry space. Avoid putting cans directly onto a concrete floor where the cans can pick up moisture. To avoid this, simply place cardboard or plywood under the cans. If cans get wet, rust may form on the metal. So if your cans get wet, take the time to dry them with a towel before storage. Toss out any can you find leaking. It means that the rust has reached the food, and allowed air into the sealed container which spoils the content. High temperatures will also shorten the shelf life of your cans. Ideally, you want to keep the temperature range from 40 degrees to 70 degrees.

Another way you can keep your cans longer is coating the containers in a very thin layer of paraffin wax. Or you can try dipping them into a solution made of one quart mineral spirits and one-eighth pound of jelly wax. Heat the mineral spirits in a can by placing it in a bucket of hot water. After dissolving the wax, dip the can with its label into the solution. Make sure the whole can is covered and then place it on wood blocks to dry. Choose a low humidity day for this task and be sure to do it outside. Of course, you don't have to do this and can simply store it on the shelf, but if you never want to let a single can go bad, this process is known for preserving the cans from moisture so you will never get rusty cans again. Canned goods should be turned over each 3 months to 6 months. This keeps solids from settling to the bottom. Cans of different ingredients will help you have some variety with your meals.

Did you know that dried food lasts a long time?

When I say dried food, I'm talking about jerky, powders, dried vegetables, dried fruit, nuts, and etc. This group of food loves a clean and dry cupboard and can last an amazingly long time.

Dried vegetables can be stored for up to 6 months or more in good conditions. Dried vegetables also have the benefit of being more flavorful, and they can be plumped up with water. Dried vegetables are more for flavoring dishes than filling them out while your canned supply is for making the dish hearty. This is exactly why I keep both fresh and dried daikon because a bit of the dried daikon adds so much flavor to soups, while the fresh daikon will be used as a filling vegetable. Dried seaweed can last for 5 or more months when stored in a dry space and add a great sea-fused taste to different meals. I have a big collection of dried goods such as dried bamboo shoots, dried fruit jerky, dried lotus roots, dried daikon, and dried tomatoes. Most of those items will last me 6 or more months.

Dried fruits will last in a closed dry container for as long as it looks and smells good. Hence they're known for lasting years in the conditions they like. Ideally, when you buy them, repack them loosely in a clean glass jar. Heat them for 20 minutes at 150 degrees and then seal them properly. This will protect them from bugs and spoiling.

Nuts last amazingly well without much effort and can be used as a snack or an ingredient. They can be stored for anywhere from 6 months to more, depending on the nut itself. Dry nuts like almonds, peanuts, and walnuts tend to keep longer than nuts that hold water like cashews. If you enjoy nut milks, you can soak your nuts overnight, blend them with filtered water, and strain it to make fresh nut milks. Cashew milk is quite yummy. You do want to drink it all within a day or so if you're storing at room temperature.

• • • •

MEAT JERKY IS ONE OF the few ways to store meat long-term besides canning it. Store it somewhere dry and away from pests and it might last for a month or more. There have been many times I left it in a hiking backpack and completely forgot about it until my next hike. Jerky can also be used as a seasoning by soaking it in good drinking water for 10 to 15 minutes before adding it to your stew. Meat won't be the main part of the meal, but it will give a great flavor boost. The soft jerky tends to hold more fats so they can spoil faster. Each brand has a different shelf life so I would pay close attention to each pack as I learn which one keeps best. A simple way to keep track of this is writing down the date of purchase onto the packet. When jerky goes bad, it grows a white mold. Look closely because sometimes the fat of the jerky is white. When you touch it, if it's solid, it's fat and if it puffs out spores, it's mold.

Powders will last well if stored on a dry counter. My favorite powder is Agar agar, which is a seaweed that is ground into flakes or a powder. I use it to make vegan jello, and the jello will set without refrigeration. It also stays firm longer and doesn't melt from heat, making it perfect for Hawaii. A small bottle of powdered agar agar has lasted me half a year easily, and whenever I have leftover fruit, I can whip it into a jello within five minutes of cooking. This makes a wonderful coffee jello too. With a supply of canned fruit, you're set for jello for half a year to a year since I've had one bottle last me 12 months before. Of course, we were not having jello every day for it to last this long, but you get the idea. Cornstarch, yeast, and baking powder will also last well in ideal conditions. Instead of buying tea bags, I invested in powdered matcha tea so I can make my own green tea lattes, and that bag of powdered tea has lasted me two years. Powdered milk also lasts much better than its fresh counterpart. I keep a bag of powdered coconut milk for drinks, and I use canned coconut milk when I want to use its oil. In fact, I make a local Hawaiian dessert called Haupia, which is made from agar agar and a can of coconut milk. But if I don't have a can of coconut milk on hand, I could easily make it out of only powdered ingredients. The world of powders is vast and can be very useful in long-term food storage because it is one of the best lasting food items that need zero refrigeration.

One of my favorite useful powders is vegan egg replacer, which is a mix of different starches. When combined with water and left to thicken, this powder is a wonderful replacement for eggs in many dishes. I love fresh eggs, and my family can easily go through a dozen in a few days, so there are times when I'm left without eggs to use for my baking needs. The answer I found is the egg replacer, which keeps well in a dry dark area and has lasted me for 6 months per box. I can even prepare it in different ways for recipes that call for egg whites, egg yolks, or whole eggs. It does not have the taste of eggs, but in most recipes, it will behave as an egg does. I have used it for pancakes, baked goods, burger patties, custard, pudding, and other recipes.

Wheat gluten is an interesting powder which can be used to make a meat replacement when combined with different flavor broths. This ingredient stores easily for 6 months when kept dry, dark, and cool. It's a natural part of flour where the starch has been removed with water, and all that remains is the stuff that makes bread chewy. I use a vegan beef broth to give it a beefy taste and then steam it for 30 minutes. After it cools, I then bread it and fry it as a nugget. You can also slice it into any shape you want, coat it in BBQ sauce, and serve it as is. Even if you're not vegan, this ingredient can help satisfy the meat cravings when you run out of jerky or canned meats. It's an item worth learning how to work with. In fact, I was scared to use it for such a long time because I had no idea what I was doing. To help you out, in the back of the book will be recipes using different items I discuss in the book so hopefully, you'll give it a try.

Flour isn't included in the powder section because to store it right is completely different from other powders. Flour doesn't like it damp, but due to its very nature, it will absorb all the water in the air and cause the paper bag it's in to mold quickly, but at the same time, it doesn't want to be exposed to light or air. When you buy it, it's best to immediately repack them into clean dry metal or glass containers and seal with airtight lids. My research has also indicated that the nutrition value is lost very quickly despite how well you can store it so it's a hard call to make. Personally, I love making things out of flour, so I've chosen to keep storing it as a major pillar of my food plan. The best way to store bulk flour is to buy a special food storage bucket which has a hand pump for sucking out all the air and sealing the flour. Otherwise, the air in any container you put it in will cause mold to form on the surface level. You can find them online, but they're not very affordable.

Storing the sweeteners well.

I ENJOY SUGAR AND IT does store well if kept dry. Keep your sugar in a dry container. I like glass jars for my sugar. Be aware not to allow your sugar to get wet or it will turn into a sticky fermented mess. Yes, it is possible for sugar to go bad if allowed to get damp.

However, honey stores better and is sweeter, measure for measure, than sugar. Baked goods last longer when you use honey instead of sugar. Local Hawaiian honey is also delicious. So how does one store their honey? If you have pure honey, keep it in covered containers in a cool, dark, and dry place. It's best to keep it covered because honey tends to pick up other odors and will lose its own scent otherwise. Over time, stored honey will darken and grow stronger in flavor, but it will not spoil. There's a story of honey discovered in an ancient Egyptian tomb that was still edible.

Pure honey usually becomes granulated as it ages or if stored at cold temperatures. This is a very natural aging process that does not affect the honey's usability. To bring it back to a liquid form, place your jar of honey in a pan of warm water. If the granules are stubborn, you can put the jar on a steamer and place the pan over low heat. Make sure that the bottom of your jar isn't directly touching the hot pan to avoid a break. Watch it carefully because you can overheat your honey, which will cause the honey to change color and flavor.

For our purposes, I highly recommend that you buy pure honey. Avoid diluted honey if you can. This is honey which has been diluted with water or any other liquid and this type of honey should be kept covered and in the refrigerator. That is because it is a syrup which can ferment or mold quickly if not kept cold. In another section of the book, I will include recipes so that you can see how to use honey in baking plus other fun things to do with your honey.

Chapter 4: The Snack Trap We all fall into sometimes

CHIPS AND CRACKERS will store well. They can be bought in bulk and will store for 6 months to a year. Now, this is going to be tricky because most families have a see-food relationship with chips and snack foods, where when they see it, they eat it. So how do you store something that will be devoured on sight?

You keep a small snack supply up close to the family while your main bulk of that item is kept far from their reach. When they're done with their supply, wait and bring up more within a time frame such as every 2 weeks, you bring up 2 bags of BBQ chips. This way, you can plan out your family's snacking. This may require having a locked box for these items because we all know how well kids can search when it comes to their favorite snacks. Stay strong and don't give in to their demands. When you first start this plan, it's a good idea to discuss it as a family about your plans. Get everyone to agree to a number of snacks per week. Then enforce it consistently.

This will help them and you grow as a person. Snacking endlessly will give them a taste for overly salty items and doesn't give them the nutrition they need to grow. But let's be real, it weighs heavily on the wallet. It's a bad habit that costs a lot to maintain. It's not impossible to store for snacking but it requires rules to limit intake.

What's interesting about snacks is that what we're addicted to is the taste of the first bite. It's not really food because it's barely there. A chip is so small when you compare it to any other food. What makes a snack so great is how flavorful it is in that first bite.That experience is what makes us all crave it and reach for it. Think about that for a while.

All of my favorite snacks memories are about those first fresh bites. So snacking is possible and easy with long-term food storage but you're going to have to get used to saying no because if they know it's there, others will ask for an advance on their snacks every chance they get. A fun way to work around this is to make one of my kids the snack master, and they get to check the food schedule to let the others know where the next delivery will come. When it's time for more snacks, the snack master helps me bring them out. When my youngest gets older, I'll have them take turns being snack master. It takes me out of the situation, and it becomes a fun game for the little ones.

Drinks can be stored for years, but if we were to be honest with ourselves, they'll never make it that long because of how fast we drink them. It's worth counting up the monthly cost of your drinks and seeing if there are any changes you'll want to make there. Because at the end of the day, drinks won't feed your family. They're fun and easy but they're not food.

Juices can be used in making desserts and other items, but we rarely use soda in our cooking. Growing up, my parents didn't do drinks besides their attempt at milk. There was always a chilled pitcher of water in the fridge, and we all drank from it. When it was empty, we refilled it with tap water, and back in the fridge it went. School is where I discovered chocolate milk and vending machines was my first soda experience. When I reached my teen years and started making my own money, I became obsessed with Dr Pepper. Most of my first paychecks went to soda and movies. When I got older, I switched to coffee and then to tea. Now I drink coconut water, fruit juice, and water.

Because my family had a strong water habit, it wasn't hard for me to go back to water. My partner, on the other hand, came from a family that never drank water. Their fridge boasted 5 different 24 packs of sodas for each person's favorite, and they refilled this every time it went low. Reframing his thoughts on the drink and the awful side effects it was having on his body helped him change the habit.

• • • •

Steps to a soft stop:

I LIKE TO DO WHAT I call a soft stop. It's when I cut back on a habit slowly until it becomes easy for the habit to fade out. What does this actually look like in practice?

Let's say I was drinking 5 cans of soda a day. I would start cutting it down to 4 cans and one bottle of water to replace that can. Then in a week, I would cut back to 3 cans and two bottles of water a day. Then in another week, I would cut down to 2 cans a day and more water. In another week, I'll be down to one can a day with mainly water as my choice drink. At this point, instead of drinking 35 cans a week, I'm down to 7 cans a week. From here, I could easily shift to a can every two days. Once I'm comfortable with that, I can make it a can of soda every three days.

The key to the soft stop is not to freak yourself out with a cold turkey approach. If you think you're never going to drink soda again, most of the time, people will freak out and say it's impossible for them. I mean if I was drinking 35 cans a week, it would seem very hard to me too. But by the end of my efforts, I was only drinking 7 cans a week. In a few more weeks, that number would be close to 3 cans a week. Once it gets down to a can per week, it doesn't seem so impossible. I mean I'm only drinking it four times a month.

This is how you take a habit and fade it out. As long as you don't increase the amount, it doesn't matter how long it takes. Just feel comfortable with the cut back and then cut back more when you're ready. At some point, it won't feel so important, and that's when you can easily stop. If I'm now drinking a can of soda every week, that means I went from drinking 120 cans of soda to 4 cans monthly. Yes, it took me four months to get to this point, but that's okay. It's still an incredible feat, and my body is still very grateful for the change I made. In a year that means I went from 1440 cans to 48 cans. At that point, it'll be a breeze for me to cut it out completely.

You can do this with any snack food that you want to eat less of. The key is to trick yourself into thinking you're only letting go of that first can. Once you agree to that, it gets easier to agree to let go of another can. Step by step, walking towards a simple goal and you'll be there before you know it.

These are the basic non-perishables of my food supply, and you may have other items that I didn't mention here.

Read up on the proper storage of any item you intend to store. If it's worth throwing money at, it's worth reading up on.

When you buy food, where does the money come from? It came from a trade of time and effort to earn that money. If you're able to retain more of the value of your purchases, it's like getting a raise in your job because you won't have to trade more time for less. So yes, you will have to put in time and effort to learn how to manage your food supply.

Chapter 5: How hard can shopping be?

Like I've said before, half of the food supply battle is fought in the kitchen while the other half is fought in the stores. These stores are designed to confuse you when you want in. It tempts us to browse the aisles like bookstores and snatch up whatever catches our eye.

Instead of having a large variety of ingredients, I aim for a deep supply of a handful of essentials.

Now, our shopping strategy is to bulk up on three non-perishables per shopping trip while you're building your supply. Each item will cost a lot because it's a 6 months or 12 months supply. So I highly recommend starting with one of each from oil, spice, and grain.

Here's an example of what I started with. I bought 6 large bottles of olive oil, 5 large shakers of a salt/garlic/pepper blend, and a 40lb bag of rice. This wasn't cheap, but I still had enough to buy the other ingredients I liked to have on hand like potatoes and carrots. On my next shopping trip, I focused on other spices and canned foods, and within a few months, my food supply was stocked.

Of course, I had to cut back on my fresh meats, drinks, snacks, and sweets for those months, but I didn't go cold turkey on it. I just cut back on all of them. Instead of 4 family size bags of chips, I bought 2. Instead of buying 5 packs of coconut water, I bought 2. I understood what was more important to stock up on, so it was easy for me to redirect the funds.

I was spending the same amount of money every month, but now I was spending 60% on non-perishables and 40% on perishables. So, my food supply was growing steadily. If you're serious about having a food supply built up quickly, I would suggest switching your funds to 80% non-perishables and 20% on perishables for a few months.

A few dollars off goes a long way when you're

buying in bulk.

SINCE YOU'RE BUYING a lot of one item, it's worth looking into coupons and deals on that one item. An example from my own life is I wanted to buy my olive oil, but the store I normally buy at had them at full retail price while another store had a sale, which would save me $5 per tin. Since I'm buying 6 tins at once, it saved me $30 to buy from the other store. There are different apps that will do the price comparison for you nowadays, and you can plan your shopping around that.

That $30 helped me buy more seasoning for my supply. When you're buying in bulk, a few dollars difference matters. Let's say I'm buying 20 cans of soup, and I normally pay $3 per can, which means my usual budget is $60 for these cans. If somehow I find a coupon that makes it $2 per can, I would save $20 by using that coupon, which means I can buy 10 more cans if I wanted to. Even a $0.50 discount would save me $10 at 20 cans. Imagine how much I would save if I found a coupon that allowed me to buy them at $1.50 instead of $3. I would be able to buy 40 cans, which would make my 6-month supply into a full year supply, and all I did was shop around for a better deal before I bought.

Pro-tips for getting in and out of the stores:

SHOPPING SEEMS EASY to do but is hard to do because of all the mini-decisions you have to make in such a short time. So here are my pro-tips for shopping with ease and for maximum benefits. First, make as many decisions as possible before you step into the store. Write down on a piece of paper which bulk items you're buying at the top of the list and then the other items you want under them. Keep this paper in your pocket or purse and pull it out as you enter the shop. Keep it in hand so that you don't just start mood shopping. Once inside, turn on a playlist on your phone and put in some earphones. This will help you focus on your goals and put you in a better mood too. Collect all your bulk items in your cart first before you shop for the perishables. Also put your bulk items on the belt first before your other food so that you can stop the cashier if your total is running too high and return your less important items before they ring them up.

You're going to be tempted to just run a higher bill while you're building your food supply, but it's not worth it because chances are high that you'll still be wasting a lot of food and you won't learn how to do more with less fresh food. Keep your budget the same but change your shopping and eating habits to more non-perishables food items.

Is that membership worth it?

Bulk stores like Costco and Sam's Club are great for building up your food supply at a lower price but make sure you know how long each item lasts, and it also helps to have lots of self-control in those places since everything is such a great deal that most people overspend. My mom is infamous for this. She always says I'm just going in to grab a roasted chicken and a pack of beer, but when she comes out, her cart is overflowing with over $300 worth of stuff. So it's better to pay $35 for that chicken and beer at the grocery store than save $15 on the chicken while spending three hundred dollars on food that won't last long and won't fit your fridge. But if you're in and out with your bulk items, there is nothing that will save you more money faster than a Costco membership.

Farmer's market can provide a steady source of fresh produce.

For fresh produce, I would suggest visiting your local Farmer's markets. The produce will be at its freshest and it will help support your local farmers. It's also great to meet farmers in your local area and put a face to the products. I've also been able to find great deals on organic vegetables. All it takes is asking them a simple question about their growing process. If they buy from elsewhere, it's most likely Costco produce (which is still a good choice, but at that point, might as well buy it from Costco yourself and save on the difference.)

Here are my Farmer's market tips: Going very early will give you the best selection, and sometimes people will give you a deal for being their first shopper of the day. If there aren't a lot of stalls, take the time to visit each stall first to get a gauge on prices and growing practices. Then, pick one stall to do most if not all of your shopping at. When you buy a lot at one stall, the farmer tends to give you extra vegetables or will cut you a better deal. If you buy one item from each stall, most likely they will charge you full retail at each stall.

Another strategy which I've used many times before is to go to the Farmer's market late, about 30 minutes before it closes. The selection will be slim, but the farmers will be more inclined to cut you a deal on anything you buy because they don't want to pack it up and carry it home. Again, do your best to bundle your shopping with one stall. There have been a few times that I got there so late that there were stalls that had already packed up and were ready to leave so they gave me all their damaged produce. I got 5 heads of cabbage for free one time!

As you buy regularly from a stall, the farmers will start giving you discounts. Now that we've talked about how to shop for your new food plan, we'll get to the next step. You know how long your food items will last because you've done the research. You have the experience of buying your food in bulk and how to redirect your funds. Now the food is here, and you have to prepare a space to store them.

Chapter 6: Where do I store all this?

If you have cupboards and closets, you're set to store 90% of your food supply. If you don't have that, a cupboard box on a metal shelf in a dry covered space will do. As you unpack each item, put them in an area assigned to them. Avoid placing canned food directly on concrete floors in a cool place since they can pick up moisture and rust. Putting down cardboard or wood under the cans will prevent this. Give each category its own space, and you'll be able to assess your supply at a glance. For items you intend to store for a full 6 months or more, write the date down on each item.

This is critical when you're first starting out. It'll give you feedback on how well you're storing your food and if you need to change anything.

You can keep your 6 months food plan on a clipboard and mark off which items you've brought, how much you've brought, and when you brought them. I like to keep my food plan on a clipboard next to the pantry. Here are some basics to keep in mind as you prepare your storage system.

Tips: The better quality of food you buy, the longer they will store. Always aim for the best grade of food you can when buying.

Metal storage cans or heavy plastic containers with airtight lids are necessary. You can also save glass jars and bottles from other food items like pickles and sauces. Once they're clean and dry, fill them up right away. Don't let empty bottles remain unused.

The best storage areas are easy to access, provide enough space, and provide temperature, moisture, and pest control.

Food keeps best in a range of temperature of 40 degrees to 60 degrees.

Food rotation is important to minimize food waste and also lets you know if you actually should be storing that item. If you don't use it within 3 months, what are the chances of you using it when you need to? If you noticed that you always have this one item left behind, consider taking it off the food storage list. Sometimes I buy things that I think might be good, but I don't use them, and they take up space that can be assigned to food I actually eat.

I recommend that you assign a shelf for older supply at eye level and below it, you store your new supply. I named the shelf I keep the older supply on my “Eat” shelf. I made this shelf my go-to when I'm cooking. The new supply stays on the lower shelf that I call the “Store” shelf. By making it harder to see, this will keep me from accidentally using the newer purchases. When my “Eat” shelf runs low, move items up from the “Store” shelf. And when I'm about to go shopping, I move everything on the “Store” shelf up to the “Eat” shelf. When I get home, I stock the “Store” shelf with my new food.

That's all you have to do to have a food rotation system; it doesn't have to be complicated. The key points are that you use the older supply first by keeping them on the “Eat” shelf, you move your “Store” shelf up to the “Eat” shelf when it runs low, and when you buy new food, you keep them on the “Store” shelf. As your food supply grows, your “Eat” shelf will stay the same while your “Store” shelf gets bigger.

Now that you've unpacked them onto the shelves, consult with your storage research, and make sure that most items are in fair if not the best storage conditions.

Proper rotation can make or break your food plan

A FUNDAMENTAL FACTOR in any successful storage system is the rotation of supplies. This will prevent spoilage and minimize the loss of food value and flavor. Most importantly though, this will get you and your family's taste buds used to the food you've stored. After his experience following World War II, Dr. Norman Wright, of the British Food Ministry, indicated people are more likely to reject unfamiliar or distasteful food during times of stress. So get them used to the food items you're storing before times of stress.

The motto that I follow is "Store what you eat and eat what you store."

As you do more shopping, keep an eye on which foods are getting closer to the end of their shelf life and plan to use them first. The chart of what you have will come in handy for this part.

Chapter 7: Signs that your food is going bad

A MAJOR FACTOR OF FOOD storage that most people don't talk about is how you can tell when food has gone bad. For each food item, the signs will be different. You can learn what good food looks like and compare it to bad food. I will give you some basic signs to look for to get you started.

Oil will get cloudy and have a strong smell when they go rancid. Some oils go cloudy from the cold like coconut oil so look for the strong smell and bad taste.

Mold is a good sign that the food has gone bad. This can grow on jerky, sauce, dried vegetables, herbs, cheese, and bread. Do not eat mold. If you find it on your food, chances are high that the spores are in all the other parts of the food item already. Of course there are exceptions to this rule, but for the most part, if you find a lot of mold, it's best to let the whole thing go.

Cans should not leak at all, and if they're rusty, you can still eat the contents if the rust hasn't reached the food inside. If your cans are rusty, the space you've put them in is too wet, and sometimes moisture can form on the cans from condensation alone. So pay attention when you handle the cans if they feel damp or not.

Sauces will lose their flavor and go sour, so a taste test will usually answer your doubts. Another good trick is to look for bubbles forming inside the sauce. If it's bubbling, you can safely assume that the sauce is fermenting. Also, when you're opening a bottle of old sauce, look for mold growing on the inner sides. If there is only mold on the lid and mouth, you can clean it. Exposure to air caused the sauce on the outside to grow mold, but if the inside is mold-free, then you can still eat it if it passes the taste test.

Vegetables will go soft, rot, and change colors as they spoil. Some will turn bitter and others will gain spots. The key to this is to remember how it looked when you first bought it and how much it has changed.

Milk will sour and clump. It also has a strong smell to alert you of spoilage. Fresh meat will turn gray and it will also smell very bad. The spoiled smell is very different from the smell of blood.

Old fried chicken will produce an oily discharge when it goes bad. For most of these things, the taste test gives clear answers and a very little amount doesn't usually bother the stomach. If it looks bad, let it go. If it's questionable by smell, it might be worth it to sample it. I don't know about you but my process for checking food for spoilage starts with a look over with my eyes. I look for changes such as bugs, mold, or anything else. Then I smell the food and if it smells sour, I throw it away. If it still smells edible, I nibble on a very small piece. If it passes the taste test, I may try a few more pieces. I'll normally stop and wait 15 minutes to see if my stomach is having a reaction to the food in any way. If it's still good at this point, I assume it's safe to eat and will eat it. If the food fails the test on any level, it goes into the trash.

Chapter 8: How long does produce last?

• • • •

HOW TO MAKE YOUR FRESH food last longer: Proper storage of any food item will make it last longer, and since fresh food goes bad faster, it is wise to learn how to store them well.

Different vegetables will all have different conditions in which they thrive. Learn which vegetables you use from your lists and research each of those vegetables. I'll give you a lot of tips on how to store a handful of common vegetables, but this book is not going to include a lot of different varieties because it is based mainly on the vegetables that I have personally worked with. Never assume what a vegetable might need unless you're willing to waste them over and over again.

It's worth the time it takes to look it up and write it down on your storage research sheet so that when you buy it, you know how to keep it. I'll share some of my research but chances are high that you have different ingredients from me. So it's best to learn how to do the research for your local items as soon as possible. I offer my humble knowledge on the vegetables I like to eat.

From what I've learned, there are two groups of vegetables: the ones that like it dry and the ones that like it damp.

Let's talk about the dry ones first since they're easier to store.

Cabbage

MY FAVORITE FOOD SECRET is cabbage can last 2 months or more if stored well. They prefer to sit on your counter or in your cupboard in a brown paper bag. They don't want to be wet or cold at all. When you're preparing the cabbage, peel the leaves off by hand instead of cutting into the whole vegetable. Toss away the dry leathery outer leaves and use the crisp leaves instead. The cabbage lasts best when it stays as close to its natural state as possible. When you cut into the vegetable, you're exposing the inner leaves to air which will cause it to go bad faster. The outer leaves will protect the inner core if left to do its job. A cut cabbage only has a lifespan of a week at most in the fridge while a cabbage that has been peeled will continue to live on the counter for months.

If for some reason, the outer leaves get wet, simply peel them off and inner leaves will be dry. Spots of rot can occur if the cabbage somehow gets splashed. When this happens, use a dry paper towel and wipe the rotten part away. Allow it to dry again and store it away from water. The worst spot for the rot to start is in the stem itself. When this happens, cut the stem as close to the body as possible, and watch closely. If the stem continues to rot away towards the center of the cabbage, despite your efforts to keep it dry and clean of rot, go ahead and use the whole vegetable. If you have bugs that can burrow into the vegetable, put it into a brown paper bag and tape it shut. A ziplock bag is the last resort but will work for a short time. The plastic will lock in the moisture and cause the vegetable to melt whatever the water touches. Light does not seem to bother the cabbage at all.

Onions

ONIONS ARE ANOTHER vegetable that loves being kept dry, so keep them hanging in your food pantry on a hook, and they will go the distance for you. To have them last, keep them in their natural state as long as possible and only cut into them if you intend to use the whole thing. The half that you cut with the roots will last longer than the half without roots. Once you cut them, if you throw them in the fridge, they might have a few days left to be of use. This is why I usually go for bags of onions where there are many little ones instead of a couple of huge onions. The little ones are the perfect size for most of my dishes, and I don't have to cut into any that won't go instantly into the pot. Light doesn't seem to have much of an effect on them, but do not let them get damp. They will start to sprout which is not necessarily a bad thing for some vegetables, but for onions, they'll eat their bulb to help the sprout. This affects the taste and texture of the onion, making it less ideal to cook with. If you wait too long after sprouting, the onion will not be suitable for cooking.

Garlic

GARLIC IS SIMILAR TO onions in storage and sprouting. They prefer to be kept dry and will consume themselves when they get damp and start sprouting. Their papery wrapping protects them from moisture in the air, so when I use them for cooking, I don't peel more than I need. I keep them in their natural form while pulling the right amount of cloves. They can keep for months on end if kept nice and dry, and it's hard to beat fresh garlic's impact in a dish. This is one item that will enjoy hanging on a hook in the kitchen.

Eggplant

EGGPLANT WILL STORE well on a counter and doesn't need any special attention as long as you keep them dry. When they go bad, they'll melt completely away. If you cut them open and the seeds are turning black, they're still edible but may have a bitter taste. It's a sign of getting old, not spoiling. In ideal conditions, they can last up to 2 weeks or more.

Cauliflower

CAULIFLOWER LIKES IT on a dry counter and can last for 2 to 3 weeks. Of course, you have to shave off the black spots, and there are people who say that the taste suffers when they're older, but honestly, I haven't tasted much of a difference. They're a great main ingredient in many dishes, and I use them in my stir-fry often. Keeping them in paper bags has helped them last longer.

••••

Tomatoes

TOMATOES PREFER TO be out on the counter instead of the fridge. The cold harms their protective skins and causes a loss of flavor while also making them spoil faster. If you can get them on the vine, they last even longer. Big tomatoes last longer than cherry tomatoes. Roma tomatoes can last for two weeks or more on a counter. The temperature in your kitchen is also a big factor in how long they'll last. They want it warm but not hot. Hot temperatures like 95 degrees and higher will speed up their spoiling considerably. In that case, the fridge will help them last the week. If your kitchen rests in a comfortable range of 85 degrees and below, they'll be fine for the two weeks. Also, removing any bad tomatoes will help the others last.

Now it's onto the vegetables that like it damp.

Potatoes and carrots, plus other root vegetables, are best stored in a sandbox. I developed this sandbox system when I started homesteading on the big island of Hawaii because they were spoiling quickly, and I didn't have access to a full-time fridge or chest freezer at the time.

This task is going to require materials, time, and elbow grease but it's an amazing tool for anyone who wants long-term fresh vegetables. This process does not require any electricity which is a super plus for anyone else living out of a cooler with ice while they're setting up their fridge. It is not a mobile solution, though, so you'll have to stay put to use this tool.

How to make your own sandbox for food storage

SO TO START, YOU'LL need a 5-gallon bucket or a 33-gallon plastic tote. A 5-gallon bucket is a small investment to start it out and will use fewer materials but it will only be able to hold a 3 lbs bag of potatoes or a 5lb bag of carrots. On the other hand, a 33-gallon plastic tote will hold up to 10lbs of vegetables easily but will cost you more materials to start. The container must have a tight-fitting lid on it so that you can keep bugs out and keep the moisture in. For my sandbox, I went with a 33-gallon tote with a waterproof lid from Home Depot and I drilled small drain holes into the side with a screen to keep the sand in while draining it of water. .

Once you have your container picked out, the next step is buying sand. If you're lucky and have access to sand, you can gather your own or you can buy sand from Home Depot. You'll need enough to fill your chosen container up to 80% of the way. I would recommend a medium-fine grade instead of rough but you don't want the sand to be powdery either. So pick a happy medium between those two extremes.

Clean the sand well by running water through it a few times. I left my plastic container with the lid off outside during a rainy week. This helps remove any dust and other things you don't want on your vegetables. Once you've washed the sand with water, spread it out on a tarp during a sunny day and let the sand dry completely before you return it back to the sandbox you've prepared. By the way, place your sandbox in a covered space designated for it because once you put the sand in, it will be incredibly heavy and hard to move.

Now you're all set for root vegetable storage. For potatoes, turnips, radishes, daikon, and carrots, dig a hole for each of the vegetables and completely cover them in sand. Any part of the vegetables that are exposed will attract bugs and rot. Now you let them be, and you're storing vegetables in your own sandbox.

How I came up with this idea

I LEARNED THIS METHOD from a home gardening book for storing vegetables during winter. I realized that I had all the materials to do it so I bought a bunch of potatoes and carrots to test out my new sandbox. Then all of a sudden, I was called away from my project and what was supposed to be a two-week Oahu visit turned into a two-month visit.

When I got home, I was upset because I didn't expect any of my potatoes to have lasted that long but to my utter surprise, not only were most of the potatoes in wonderful condition but the carrots were crispy and in better condition than the potatoes. They were also sporting beautiful green tops, and I used the carrot leaves to make a soothing tea for myself.

The sand will get moist from the vegetables releasing their water, so vegetables that like it dry will hate the warm and slightly damp conditions inside of the sandbox. You shouldn't wet the sandbox. I do live in a high humidity environment so I have never had to do this. But if the sand is very dry because you live in a dry area, it might be worth it to mist it lightly. The sand should be slightly moist but not wet. Otherwise the vegetables will produce enough wetness of their own, and the sand will keep them in a semi-alive state of growth.

Potato basics

SO WHAT'S UP WITH POTATOES? I heard that if they're green they're toxic, but if they're growing in the sandbox doesn't that make them green, hence toxic? When potatoes are exposed to sunlight, they turn green from a toxic compound created by the sunlight. If they're kept in the dark, they will develop sprouts called eyes. These eyes will shoot through the sand and turn into big beautiful leaves. The sprout and the leaves can be easily ripped off while preparing it for cooking. As long as the flesh of the potato stays white inside and the skin doesn't change color, they're safe to eat. The sprout does not affect the taste or texture of the potato. So it's something you pull off the potato which is still hard and ready for eating. If you cover them properly with sand, even opening and closing the lid won't expose potatoes to sunlight. You can go and put a potato in your window and watch it turn green. It's still alive and fine but now it's full of a compound that doesn't sit well with our stomachs. That's all. You can still take this potato and plant it and it will make white potatoes that have never seen sunlight that you can eat. The original green bulb will never lose the compound so it will always be toxic for eating but it doesn't stop it from being a plant. Fun fact is that you're free to plant the sprouts from the potatoes and if properly cared for, they will produce new potatoes of their own. Sometimes I lose a potato in a far corner and when I dig it out, the original potato is gone but it has left a couple of baby potatoes in its place. The sand has very little nutritious value so I don't recommend using it as a garden. But as a way to keep potatoes for long-term food storage, nothing has been better for me. When you cut into the potato, if it has black or gray spots in the flesh, you can cut those parts out and it doesn't affect the taste of the rest of the potato.

Remember to bury them in the sand

WHAT HAPPENS IF YOU don't bury the vegetables and just dump them on top of the sand? Well, I know this because well, I've done it. I've been so busy unpacking and putting away my other groceries that I've dumped a bag of potatoes on the sand and closed the lid. In a few weeks when I opened my sandbox to pull a couple of potatoes out, I found a mushy mess that had melted on the surface of the sand.

The sand keeps them dry enough so that they don't rot, and the tiny amount of water in the sand keeps them alive. If you don't have the sand to draw the water away, they just straight up melt in the damp conditions. Of course, I'm also talking from the point of view of doing this in Hawaii where the humidity is 75% to 95% on some days and it's hot. If you live in a cooler climate, the potatoes might have a chance just being on top of the sand but I wouldn't bet on it.

To clean up this mess, you scoop out the rotten vegetables along with the sand that is touching it. Remove all the dirty sand until you feel clean sand again. Keep the sand in a bowl and run water through it again until the sand is clean. You'll know the sand is clean when you can stir the sand and the water remains clear. Then let the sand dry completely before you return it to the sandbox. We don't throw away yucky sand. It's a rock that can be cleaned and put back. You'll have to refill the sand eventually but this is a once-every-two-year event if you take care to save your sand.

Now here are some key points to remember while using the sandbox system. Never put wet sand or dirty sand into your sandbox. Just don't do it. It will make your vegetables rot and smell awful. The magic to the system is clean, very very lightly damp sand, without it, you've got nothing. So do not rush and put soppy wet sand into your sandbox.

For most places, you don't need to wet your sandbox. The vegetables will keep it wet enough. You don't have to do anything but add more fresh vegetables if it feels a bit dry there. If for some reason the sand feels dripping wet, you can turn a heat light onto the sand with the lid off and dry it that way. Even a normal light bulb will do some drying. Even if your sand feels too dry, I would only slightly mist it once every two weeks. It's a tricky balance but it's worth learning what works best for you and your area.

Keep your sandbox free of rotten vegetables by covering them completely in the sand and removing any spoiling parts right away. This means checking on your sandbox weekly or bi-weekly at the least, more so if you're testing a new vegetable in the sandbox.

Things that like it cool and completely dry will not do well in the sandbox. So things like cabbage, onions, and garlic will hate it there.

Out of everything I've ever put in the sandbox, no one thrives in there like the carrots. I bury the carrots standing horizontally to save space, and you can have a tiny bit of the top sticking out so you can tell where they are. The tops will sprout greens that make a great tea. All you do is steep the leaves in hot water for 10 minutes, pull out the leaves, stir in sugar, and serve.

Carrots

CARROTS, LIKE MOST of the other vegetables, like to be kept in their natural form so avoid cutting them. They will be okay most of the time but sometimes the cut will get too wet and cause the whole thing to rot. If you do cut them, I find that keeping them out for a day or two so that the cut can dry. This will lessen their chance of rotting when you do put them back in. Long gone are the days when my carrots would melt away or go limp and wrinkled. Inside of the sand, in their whole form, they can stay crisp for two months and more at a time. Thin roots will shoot out the length of the carrot, but they're easy to break and don't affect the carrot's taste or texture.

Root vegetables

THE OTHER ROOT VEGETABLES that I've found that like being buried in the sandbox are daikon, turnip, and radish. As long as they stay covered, they can last for about a month or more. If there are bad parts on the roots when you buy them, cut them off and let them dry on the counter for a day or two before burying them. I highly recommend avoiding root vegetables with bruises so that you don't have to cut them. They last much better in their complete form. It saves you more money in the long run.

Celery

NOW, CELERY IS TRICKY because it doesn't want to be buried in the sand but will last longer, resting on top of the sand in the sandbox. The celery will grow upward towards the lid yet once it touches the lid, which is usually wet, it will instantly rot wherever it touches the celery. Due to this, celery can only be stored in the sandbox for two weeks or less. When you use celery, peel the outer stocks off first and leave the core alone to help it live. If you remove the core, which is the leafy parts for your recipe, that's okay but there is a risk of rot starting from the center out when you do that. Sometimes it doesn't affect the celery, and sometimes it does, so be aware of that. If you only have the leafy core left, you can put it into a small dish of water and it will keep like this for about a week. If you still have big thick stems, the core growing will cause them to yellow and melt away. So try the water dish only when you are down to the little center cluster of leaves. These leaves are great as a seasoning garish.

Leeks

LEEKS ARE SIMILAR TO celery in that you don't have to bury the whole thing but its roots like to be touching the sand. When the leaves reach the lid, it will rot. Yet, despite all this, leeks can last two or more weeks in the sandbox. To keep it longer, keep the whole plant in a cup of water in a sunny spot and they will last for about a month in that state. Remember to change the water every few days. When you use it, you can cut off the root bundle and put it in a glass of water, and it will produce more leaves. Keep changing the water, and when the roots are 2 inches, you can plant it in your garden.

Vegetables that like it wet

NOW WE'LL TACKLE A group of vegetables that like it wet. These vegetables tend to be tricky because they have short lifespans that can change based on different factors like temperature or light.

Herbs

GREEN ONIONS LIKE TO be kept in a glass of water on the counter. Sage, rosemary, Thai basil, and mint also enjoy this kind of treatment. They will sprout more roots and be ready for planting after you pick off all the leaves and use them in cooking. I've kept fresh herbs like this on my counter for a week or so. If you have a freezer, freezing herbs help them last, yet dried herbs last just as long and have as much taste without the need for electricity. When I have fresh herbs, I like to keep them very fresh.

Greens

SURPRISINGLY, LETTUCE'S roots like to sit in cold, shallow water but this will help it last for 3-4 days if you leave them on the counter, buy when you intend to use within a few days. In a fridge, they can last a week, and if you're lucky maybe two weeks. This one has been tricky for me since my partner loves salads and only likes lettuce, but without a fridge, I've wasted a lot of heads playing around with the right storage method. The best thing I've found for them is to be kept cold and in some water at the base, yet I've never made them last longer than a week without refrigeration.

Kale

KALE, ON THE OTHER hand, is hardy and will easily last a week in room-temperature water. Keeping them in water on a counter will also keep them firm. Like most vegetables, the more you cut them, the more areas for bacteria to attack and spoil. So a cut bag of kale will often only last a few days in the fridge and less on the counter. If possible, buy kale still intact with its stems.

What to do with fruit

I DON'T KNOW ABOUT your family but I have a couple of monkeys for daughters and they demand fruits daily. I usually keep all my fruit at room temperature in their natural form. Cut fruit will spoil faster unless kept chilled so it's better to cut it when you're ready to eat.

Strawberries

STRAWBERRIES SHOULD be eaten in one or two days because they will not last without refrigeration while left on the counter. Even in the fridge, it's amazing how fast they can go moldy within a few days. Frozen, they will last months.

Apples

AS YOU MAY ALREADY know, apples are great when it comes to long-term storage. Keep them dry and clean. Don't cover them and allow them to breathe because they emit a lot of gasses which if trapped will quicken their spoiling. Eat the apples with bruises and bad spots first to help the others keep better. That old saying about a bad apple spoils the bunch is correct thanks to the gasses they emit. I've had a bag of apples for two to three months. Of course, they usually don't make it that long since my daughters eat them so fast.

Oranges

ORANGES CAN OUTLAST apples when it comes to storage. With that thick protective skin, they like to be stored dry in a hung-up bag. Make sure the bag is not made of plastic and go for a breathable fabric. A bag of oranges can last two to three months. Keep an eye out for bugs burrowing into them and spoiling them quickly. I like to keep my burlap sack bags that have a zipper on top for orange storage because it's breathable while also sealing them away from pests.

Bananas

BANANAS ARE WELL-LOVED in my family but when it comes to storage, they're okay. How long they can last all depends on if they're green or yellow when you buy them. If they're already yellow, leave them uncovered on the counter and they will last about two weeks. You can eat them with brown and black spots on them.

Even if the flesh inside is mushy and brown, you can still eat them. In fact, I normally mash them up, mix them with egg and flour, and pan fry them to make banana pancakes. Now if they're green, they'll last up to a month before they turn yellow. If you want them to turn yellow quickly, put them in a paper bag and the gas they produce will quicken the ripening process to about a week or two.

Since there are many different varieties, this estimate is for apple bananas (common local variety in Hawaii) and Cavendish bananas. Bananas don't like being in the fridge and tend to turn brown quickly, but they can be frozen to last for months, but all frozen bananas will naturally brown and won't look nice for many desserts.

Pears

PEARS CAN BE KEPT ON a dry counter and they'll last for about two weeks at most. In the fridge, they may last about two to three weeks and frozen, they'll last months. Don't put them in the fridge and then leave them out since their protective skin is now damaged by the cold. When you're buying, make sure to pick out harder ones because they're younger. The soft ones are older and will spoil quickly.

Nectarines

NECTARINES CAN BE KEPT on a dry counter and will last three weeks that way. As with the pears, when you're shopping, make sure to pick out hard, younger fruit. They enjoy room temperature storage.

Grapes

GRAPES PREFER STAYING dry and on a counter, they can last about a week and a half. In the fridge, they can last longer, about two weeks but soon they'll get moldy. Dried grapes in the form of raisins last a great deal longer than their fresh counterparts and you can plump them back up in water. The water will taste a little like juice and the grapes have an interesting transparent look to them.

Kiwis

KIWIS CAN LAST SURPRISINGLY long without refrigeration. On the counter, I've had them last for a month. Their fuzzy skin protects them, so eat any kiwis that are cut or broken. They will soften as they ripen, getting sweeter. The flesh inside should stay a bright color and when the flesh is brown, you can still eat them but they become sour as they go bad.

Plums

PLUMS ARE GREAT FOR storage and can last for three weeks on a dry counter. Keeping them dry and clean will help them stay sweet and yummy. In the fridge, they can last up to a month and a half easily and frozen, they can last much longer.

Pomegranate

POMEGRANATES ARE AMAZING. They can store for a month or more thanks to its thick skin. They prefer a dry counter with nothing covering them. As they dry, the skin will harden and wrinkle but the seeds inside will not be affected. Once you pop the skin, eat it within the week.

The secret to fresh produce

THE KEY TO STORING your fresh produce is checking up on them weekly to eat up overly ripe ones and damaged ones. This will also alert you of any pests you need to safeguard them from. If something is slimy, remove it and clean up anything that has been touched by the rot with a paper towel.

Chapter 9: How should I store other items?

Vegan perishables:

Pickled goods can be tricky since some will last for some time while others tend to have a short lifespan. It will completely depend on what vegetables are used and what type of pickling was done. If you have refrigeration, most pickled items will last very well for you, but they still often only have a shelf life of a few months. Items such as pickles and kimchi will sour depending on how much air is in their jar. It's best for you to do your research and record your results. If you don't have a fridge, once you open a jar of pickles, you have a week before it spoils. The water will become cloudy, and the pickles will taste gross. Kimchi, on the other hand, has lasted me three weeks without refrigeration. Why is this so when they're both pickled items? I have no idea. So for this part, it's best to open it, write down the exact date of opening, eat what you want, and then write down the exact day it went bad. Different brands use different pickling mixtures, giving each product different spoiling rates. Homemade pickled items tend to last longer, but that makes sense since they're fresh.

Tofu is a great ingredient if you buy it in boxed packaging. Tofu in plastic containers must be refrigerated and will spoil within two weeks. Boxed tofu, packaged in waxy cardboard material, will last on your shelf for a year. Make sure there are no rips or leaks when buying them. Different firmness variations serve different dishes.

Plant milks last a year in their original packaging, with boxed options being a better long-term storage solution than those in plastic containers. Nut milks in powdered form store twice as long and take up less space. Be cautious not to tear the packaging as it may lead to spoiling.

Vegan cheese lasts as long as its dairy counterpart. Daiya brand vegan cheese blocks last longer than shredded, and proper refrigeration helps prevent mold growth. Observation reveals that an unopened bag of shredded cheese can last up to two months. Yet as with all cheese, once it gets moldy, it's over.

The next perishables on the list are all animal products. If this topic doesn't interest you or your family, feel free to skip it. First, you have to understand that when a cow is killed, its body is drained of blood, and the meat is allowed to age for a week before it makes it to the store. Smaller animals have a shorter aging period. During a road trip across the US, I worked on an organic chicken and goat farm that processed 35 chickens weekly, so I got very familiar with preparing chicken bodies. For chickens, the farmer aged them by putting the bodies into an ice bath for a full day before selling them. The aging period helps the meat get softer and taste better. So when you buy meat from the store, it's already been aged and is ready for eating. Often, we buy so much that we can't eat it all at once, so the usual answer is to throw the leftover parts into the freezer and use them when you're ready. Often the frozen meat remains unused for months. Until we finally dig it out and find it has frost burn, leading to wastage. This system is not great, but many continue to follow it because it's a common practice.

I offer a simple suggestion. Buy non-perishable meat as often as you buy it fresh. Purchase canned meat, smoked meat, and jerky to add to your food supply. If you don't know how to use those ingredients, it's never too late to learn, as canned chicken is as easy to use as fresh chicken. Canned meats will last for more than six months if stored in a dry, cool, dark place. Unfrozen fresh meat in the fridge will last for about two weeks if it's fresh, while frozen meat can last a couple of months before frost burn occurs. To ensure efficiency, use your frozen meat often to prevent overbuying and waste.

If you have a pressure cooker with the right jars, you can can your own meat instead of freezing it. Once canned, meat can last on the shelf without refrigeration for years. Clean your jars by steaming them before use to kill all germs for a higher success rate. Experiment with seasoning or preserve it plain for versatility in various dishes. Make sure to label the date on the lid of the canned meat and consume it within six months. One way to save on meat is to find a local rancher and buy in on a cow. When it's time, you get your cut and you preserve it by canning your supply. Of course, you can also do this when there is a good sale at your local grocery stores.

Jerky is a great meat snack that can last a few months if kept sealed. Consider the drying technique used by different brands to determine shelf life. Jerky can be added to soups as a flavoring agent by soaking it in hot water before adding it to the pot. Chinese sausages in plastic air-sealed packages can last a long time if kept airtight but must be consumed within a few days once opened.

Milk and cheese are staples in the American diet. Growing up in an Asian household, I never understood why there was always a gallon of milk in the fridge since no one drinks it. My mom would use a little bit in her coffee from time to time, but I think she wanted my little brother and me to drink it straight. Since she and my dad didn't drink it, we never drank it that way. We begged for cereal to have with the milk, but cereal was often too expensive, so we would always have a gallon of spoiled milk in our fridge. If this is not the case in your home, I'm glad. If there is anything you're buying in hopes of people eating it and it doesn't get eaten, just stop buying that item. Explain to everyone that if you buy it again, there must be no waste of it or it goes on the "not buying" list. Yes, it will require you to talk to your family about their eating habits. If you drink milk and love it, that's wonderful. Make sure that you're buying the amount you actually use and there's no problem.

If you want to slide milk into your non-perishable list, buy powdered milk. Powdered milk stores well for years and can be used in most recipes that call for milk. In fact, you can even use it to make cheese and other dairy-based products like yogurt. It's easily used for cereal and baking. Mix up a batch and chill it in the fridge before cereal, and no one will notice the difference. There are different types of powdered milk; you can go for buttermilk or skim milk. If you're looking to replace normal milk, I would suggest trying powdered skim milk.

Cheese can last for a while before it starts getting moldy. Shredded cheese will mold faster than a block of cheese. The main key to proper cheese storage is limiting air exposure. Keeping it wrapped and covered will help it last. The more surface area for the air to touch, the more chances for mold spores to land on it and grow. That's why shredded cheese will mold so quickly. Buy blocks if you can and use a grater to get the cheese you need for your meals. Cheese lasts best in the fridge, but I've had a block of cheese kept in a dry cool spot last me about a month without refrigeration. With a block of cheese, where mold shows up, you can cut off that part and eat what's under it. This is what makes cheese such a staple; it tastes like a perishable but acts like a non-perishable. If kept well, you can easily have a block of cheese for more than a few months, but it will greatly depend on the climate you live in. Cheese during summer will behave differently than cheese during winter.

Let's talk about water and how to store it. If you grew up in the city as I did, I never realized that people even stored water. I thought it was a given that water would come out of the tap forever even in times of emergencies. That all changed when I went off-grid. Big Island, Hawaii has a unique system for water, as everyone on this island lives off rain catchment. Due to the dense lava rock that makes up the island, it is costly to get water pumped to your property for the sheer amount it costs to drill miles of pipes to reach you. Hence, most people on this island catch rainwater and filter it for drinking and daily use. The state has also opened up spring water stations, which the residents can use to fill up on their water needs, but this requires constant hauling and usually a vehicle that can handle carrying a large water tank.

I live in a rain-heavy area, so I catch my rain and filter it for drinking. A wonderful water filter that I recommend is the Mini Sawyer, which can filter up to 100,000 gallons.

It's surprising how long people can live without food, and yet when it comes to water, it's a very short time before it's harmful to our health. So don't minimize the importance of your water storage supply. Nowadays, most people will store bottled water and consider themselves done. In the long run, bottled water is a very small amount of water for how much space it will take up. It is better to get a large container and store water in that. Remember that you'll need water for preparing your dried foods and mixing with your powdered foods. Plus bathing, washing dishes, brushing your teeth, and drinking. It's one of the abundant elements of most people's lives, so we use it rather carelessly. You could say that people are water-rich and don't realize it. Go throughout your day and count how many times you actually use water, and you'll realize that a pack of 24 bottled water will be gone within a matter of hours if you were to depend on it for all your water needs.

When water is stored properly, the more stored, the better. Let's assume that the weather stays nice, you eat a low protein diet, and are only doing moderate work; you will need at least half a gallon of water per day for drinking and food preparation. So at a bare minimum, you would want to store 14 gallons of water per person for a 2-week period. For a family of four, that would be 56 gallons for 2 weeks. That's drinking water and food preparation alone. That supply isn't for bathing, washing dishes, or anything else. If you can catch rainwater for those needs, you would still need 56 gallons of drinking and cooking water. Now you can see why bottled waters won't cut it. The ability to filter water is important, but it depends on your weather, which can be fickle. If you have access to a well or river water, then you have a more stable source than people who have to pray for rain. For your health and well-being, please only use safe water for cooking, drinking, and brushing of teeth.

There are four basic methods for obtaining drinkable water from polluted water, and they are filtration, chemical treatment, freezing, and distillation. Filtration and chemical treatment are usually used in combination. When you treat the water with water purification tablets alone, the foreign particles are still floating around in there. The taste is also awful, and filtering it helps with that as well.

Boiling water is the safest method for purifying and is easy to do. Simply boil it vigorously for 3 minutes. This will destroy any bacteria within the water and make it safe for use. To help the water taste better, you can chill it and aerate it by pouring it from one clean cup to another several times. This adds air back into the water and changes the taste.

Distilling the water means boiling the water and catching the steam that comes off the pot and storing it in another container. Usually, there is special equipment to buy to do this, but I have found that you can DIY a distilling setup with tin foil and glass bowls. You can learn this on YouTube easily. The resulting water will taste better than regular boiled water.

Most people have seen water purification tablets that use chlorine or iodine, and these are easy to store and can be bought at a low cost. If you don't have these on hand, you can also use household bleach that has hypochlorite as its only active ingredient. An important side note is to make sure that hypochlorite is the only active ingredient, or you could poison your water supply. If there are any other active ingredients, do not use it. I repeat, do not use it. The most common is bleach solutions of 5.25% sodium hypochlorite. All the quantities I will recommend are based on that strength of bleach. If you have something stronger, please look up another chart for water purification.

Treating Water with a 5-6% Liquid Chlorine Bleach Solution		
Volume of Water to be Treated	Treating Clear/Cloudy Water:	Treating Cloudy, Very Cold, or Surface Water:
	Bleach Solution to Add	Bleach Solution to Add
1 quart/1 liter	3 drops	5 drops
1/2 gallon/2 quarts	5 drops	10 drops
1 gallon	1/8 teaspoon	1/4 teaspoon
5 gallons	1/2 teaspoon	1 teaspoon
10 gallons	1 teaspoon	2 teaspoons

NOW, WHAT YOU DO IS add a bleach solution to your water in a clean container.

The amount you put in will depend on two factors. One is how much water you're purifying and what condition the water is in. Please use the chart for the proper quantity.

Now you add the bleach, mix the water by stirring well or shaking the container. After you've stirred it well, let it stand for 30 minutes. After 30 minutes, the water will have a distant chlorine taste or smell, which proves it's safe for use now. If the smell or taste isn't present, add another dose of solution to the water, mix well, and let it stand for another 15 minutes.

Do not use it if there is not a smell or taste of chlorine in the water. That is a sign that the water is treated and ready for use. Time, heat, and contamination will weaken your bleach and make it not usable in this matter sometimes.

When you have clean, safe water ready for storage, you want to store it in thoroughly washed plastic containers with tight-fitting caps. Make sure that the plastic used in making the containers is of food-grade level and will not leak into your water supply. I use a 55-gallon plastic drum. Glass containers with good screw-on lids are good as well, but they store less water and can be shattered by cold or impact. Metal containers will add a taste to the water over time unlike plastic and glass.

You can bottle your water by filling up an empty bottle to within 1" of the top and pressure cooking it. Store the bottles together tightly so they don't break each other and put some padding between the bottles such as newspapers and cloth. Clean water stored this way will remain yummy and safe indefinitely. Now all you have to do is check for leaks and changes in water conditions every few months. If the water has gone cloudy or developed an unpleasant taste, discard the water and prepare another batch. This time make sure that you clean the container better. You can even pour boiling hot water over the glass bottles to kill off all bacteria after you wash it with soap and water.

I like to buy gallon-size glass jugs of apple juice, and I keep all of those jugs for water storage. If you were to buy the gallon-size glass jugs alone, they will cost about the same as the apple juice-filled ones.

When stored in clean containers and completely free of bacteria at the time of storage, water will remain safe. Most disease organisms tend to die during long storage, hence the longer the water is stored, the safer it will become. This is only true if stored properly from the start, so please remember that. If your water is going bad, the most common reason is that your container was contaminated or your water wasn't properly purified.

Tap water does not need to be purified, but rainwater, river water, and lake water need to be purified. So you can fill up with tap water and pressure cook it, and you're set.

Most people won't be able to store a year's worth of water. At a minimum, for a year, you will need at least 200 gallons per person. That amount of water will weigh about a ton and a half plus occupy nearly 200 cubic feet of space. That's for one person's drinking and cooking for a year. At most, people will be able to store a month's worth, and this will greatly depend on the size of your family. If you're living on rain catchment like me, then it is much easier to store that amount because it will be based on your tank size. With a tank of 10,000 gallons, you'll be able to have enough for a large family, but remember that 200 gallons are strictly for drinking and cooking only. If you use this amount for washing, cleaning, flushing the toilet, filling fish tanks, and watering plants, you'll be surprised at how fast 10,000 gallons can go.

• • • •

Now let's talk about Pests

NOW THERE ARE A HANDFUL of pests that will ruin your food storage, and the most common will be rodents. The real problem with these guys isn't how much they eat but how much food they'll contaminate when they're crawling around your food. Rats and mice will bite their way through cardboard boxes and plastic bags. Canned items are safe from their chewing power, so they can be left out without fear of loss. For the items they can get into, I suggest putting them into a container with a lid, such as a plastic tote. They won't be able to chew through that. I keep a pair of ratter cats, and they have done a wonderful job. In the past, I had accidentally stumbled upon a good rat trap. I hung up a bird feeder and left a bucket under it. The rain filled the bucket, and I simply left it there. The bird feeder was near a bush, and one night as I walked past the bird feeder, I noticed a lot of movement and thought to myself, what kind of birds eat at night.

Turns out the bush was a perfect climbing ladder for the local rats, and they were happy to eat up all my bird feed. As they fought over the food, they would push each other off, and once they landed in the water, they would swim until they drowned. The next day, there were four large rats in the bucket, and I dumped it out. I returned the bucket to its spot and let the rain refill it. Every couple of days, I would refill the bird feeder and dump out the bucket. This system was doing well, but I got tired of burying the bodies. So when my daughter asked for a cat, I was eager to explore new ways to keep the rat population down.

The second most common pests are bugs, and there are so many amazing varieties of them that alone can be a full book, so I won't be getting into this too much since I still struggle with this. Watch out for the grain black beetle that can hatch in your store-bought grain. The best way to keep out bugs is to keep your food in bug-proof containers and remove rotten produce quickly. If you use chemical sprays to control bugs, do your best to not spray too close to your vegetables and grains since they can impact the taste and smell of the food. Ants are very tricky to deal with and can sneak into thin cracks.

So now you're armed with knowledge about your eating habits, your shopping habits, and your storing habits. Start small and learn how to properly store a couple of items at a time. Otherwise, you'll lose food as you learn. Losing some of your supply is a part of learning so don't stress too much over it. The best way to minimize this is to work with one item at a time and keep good notes on how you're storing it, the dates, and the brands you're using. The more you know about each food item, the less mistakes you'll make overall. Have fun learning how to take care of your food and it will feed you and your loved ones well.

Chapter 10: My Favorite Recipes

Veggie noodle soup

You'll need:

6 cups of water
2 veggie bouillon cubes
1 tablespoon of dried brasil
1 tablespoon of garlic
1 tablespoon of thyme
1 teaspoon of Olive oil
1 cup of cut potatoes
1 cup of carrots
½ cup of celery
1 small onion
2 cups of pasta bowties
Salt and pepper to taste

- Heat up oil in a pot and add your dried seasoning to the warming oil.

- Over low heat, simmer the herbs until their scent is activated.

- Add water to the pot, up to the halfway mark on your pot. If you have broth on hand, you can use that instead of water.

- If you only have bouillon cubes, use water and add two cubes.

- For my usual recipe, I add 1 cup of potatoes, 1 cup of carrots, ½ a cup of celery, and a small onion. Cut them into any size you want, but I like my vegetables to be chunky.

- Add your vegetables at this point and allow them to cook until soft.

- When the vegetables are close to being done, add 2 cups of pasta bowties to the soup.

- Sometimes you'll have to add more water to cover all the ingredients if your soup has cooked down. That's okay, go ahead and add a cup at a time when it gets low.

- Cook for another 20 minutes until the bowties are soft. Salt and pepper to your taste.

- The soup is ready to serve. It will serve about 4 - 5 people.

You can easily add a can of chicken to make it chicken veggie soup. Add it in when you add the noodles.

• • • •

VEGAN LYCHEE JELLO

This is a classic and a fan favorite with my kids. Of course, if you're using regular jello, this recipe will work, but for us, we use agar agar powder. Agar agar is also available in flakes and cubes. Please read the instructions carefully to prepare. For me, I use powdered agar agar, which works very quickly.

• • • •

YOU'LL NEED:

4 cups of water
1 can of lychee
1/4 cup of sugar
2 teaspoons of Agar agar powder.

- Bring 4 cups of water to a boil in your pot.

- Add 1/4 cup of sugar, 2 teaspoons of Agar agar, and the can of lychee into the water.

- Allow the sugar and agar to fully dissolve in the boiling water for 5 minutes. Make sure that you stir and don't let the powder clump up.

- Once the agar agar dissolves, lower your heat and let it simmer for 5 minutes.

- Pour into the molds you have and leave it in the fridge for 30 minutes.

Once it sets, it's ready to serve 3-4 people.

Feel free to play around with your agar agar measurement. More will make the jello harder while less will make it softer. Another fun idea is to make your favorite drink and add agar agar to it. You can make coffee jello or black tea jello. Cut them up small and then add that jello to your drinks. Instead of fruit, you can also add a can of coconut milk, and this will make a Hawaii specialty, haupia. Also, try doing this with eggs and vanilla to make a dense custard.

A word of advice is that if you use citric fruit such as lemon, oranges, or pineapples, the agar agar will not set well due to their acids.

Vietnamese Porridge

This is my favorite lazy recipe for days when I'm not feeling up to the task of cooking.

You'll need:

2 cups of rice

8 cups of water

2 or 3 eggs

1 bouillon cube or 2 cups of broth

2 tablespoons of fish sauce
3 tablespoons of soy sauce
1 teaspoon of white pepper
Salt and pepper to your taste

- Add the 6 cups of water to a pot.

- Add the 2 cups of rice and start the fire on medium. If you have leftover cooked rice, this cuts down the cooking time by half, but do not mix cooked rice with uncooked rice. If you want to use your cooked rice and your uncooked grains, first cook the rice until it's done and then add the leftover rice.

- Once your rice is soft, add your broth cube and add 2 more cups of water. If you have any cooked rice, this is where you should add it.

- Now you'll keep your heat low and allow the rice to cook down into a mushy texture. If you run out of water before the rice is broken down, add a cup of water at a time.

- Stir often, and if the bottom is sticking, add more water.

- Once the grain completely breaks down, lightly beat your eggs in a separate bowl.

- Slowly pour in your eggs while stirring.

- Season your pot with your soy sauce, white pepper, and fish sauce.

- Season with salt and pepper.

- Turn off the heat and allow it to cool before you serve it.

This dish is easy on the stomach for people who are sick and easy on the cook. You can add to this recipe by adding browned ground meat when you add the egg. You can throw any kind of meat in there you want. Shredded chicken and ham are good choices.

Of course, you can also make it vegan by replacing the eggs with tofu and not adding fish sauce. (If you can, get the vegan fish sauce because the dish's success depends on the fish sauce taste.) You can throw in chickpeas and corn instead.

Vegan Roast

Even if you eat meat, learning how to use vital wheat gluten will help you stretch out your supply while still satisfying those cravings.

You'll need:

2 cups of vital wheat gluten

2 broth cubes of chicken or beef flavoring, (There are vegan versions of this. I like the Edwards and Sons brand.)

2 tablespoons of ketchup

1 teaspoon of Worcestershire sauce

1 ½ cup of hot water

¼ teaspoon of liquid smoke

• • • •

- Add your broth cubes, Worcestershire sauce, ketchup, hot water, and liquid smoke into a container and stir well.

- Once they dissolve, add your mixture to your vital wheat gluten and knead it like bread. The more you knead it, the denser your roast will be, and the less you work it, the more fluffy and airy it will be. I prefer it fluffy so I only knead it for about 5 minutes. You may do it for 10 minutes but avoid going too hard on the kneading because after 20 minutes, you'll have a very small and very hard roast.

• Now you'll place the wheat gluten blob into a steaming container and steam it for 30 minutes.

• After 30 minutes of steaming, turn off the fire and allow the roast to rest for 15 minutes before serving.

• Serve it with a side of mashed potatoes. This will serve 4 people.

• I like to top the roast with a brown gravy or ketchup.

VEGAN NUGGETS

If you have any leftover steamed wheat gluten, you should try this recipe.

You'll need:
2 cups of Strips of steamed wheat gluten
1 cup of flour
1 cup of bread crumbs
⅔ teaspoon of garlic powder
1 egg
Frying oil

• • • •

• Cut your wheat gluten into thin strips

• Mix the flour, the seasoning, and the egg in a bowl.

• Dip the strips into the flour mixture.

• Put the bread crumbs in a separate bowl and coat the strips with it

• Fry it in hot oil to make your own nuggets. Make sure that the oil isn't over 120 degrees or below 80 degrees.

• When the coating is golden brown, they're done.

• Set aside and allow them to cool for a few minutes, serve with ketchup, mayo, or whatever sauces you prefer.

MY DAUGHTERS LOVE THEM, and I'm sure your kids will like it too. A key trick I learned is to not mention that it's vegan until after they're done eating. Don't say anything while you're preparing them about it being new or different from other nuggets. Allow them to eat them without your input, and most of the time, kids won't even notice that. When they're full and happy, you can bring up that there was no meat in it, but that's up to you. Food is food and if they like it, why ruin that with talk of how good it was for them?

The key I've found is to not make a big deal over it being vegan or not. We never talk about how our steamed veggies are vegan; they're just a part of the meal. So why do we have to make a big deal over our nuggets being vegan? Because it's new to us, and we want to chat about the newness. And there is nothing wrong with it, but wait until the food is eaten because sometimes just the idea of something being different will cause our families to form opinions of the food before they give it a try. My younger brother is this kind of person. If I serve him something and not mention it's vegan, he'll eat it no problem, but if I tell him that it's vegan, he'll moan and complain the whole time before he ever puts a bite in his mouth.

Cabbage Omelette

You'll need:

4 eggs

A large onion

1 teaspoon of fish sauce

1 teaspoon of soy sauce

3 cloves of garlic

¼ cup of milk

5 cups of shredded cabbage.

- Cut your onion into slices, mince your garlic, and then sauté them over low in oil.

- When the onions are soft, add the cabbage.

- Season with the fish sauce.

- Continue to sauté them until the cabbage is soft, which can take about 5 minutes, but it will depend on the thickness of your cabbage.

- Crack your eggs into a new bowl and season them with soy sauce and salt/pepper.

- Add the milk to your eggs and beat them well.

- When the cabbage is soft, add the egg mixture.

- Flip your omelet in parts because it's going to get heavy.

- When it's done, plate it and garnish it with cheese (vegan/ regular is up to you).

This is a crowd-pleaser and tastes great when served over rice. This recipe is wonderful for using up your cabbage while stretching your egg supply. The recipe above serves 5 people. If you want to make it bigger, add 1 egg for each 2 cups of cabbage.

Just heads up, this is a recipe that egg-replacer powder will not be able to replace egg in. It will work, but it'll be more of a pancake than an omelet and be very bland.

Chapter 11: Let's review

You did it! You reached the end of the book and you know a lot more about food storage!

How much have you learned about how to store your food properly?

Hopefully, you feel more prepared to start this system. A good food storage system has given me so much comfort and certainty in these wild times, and my greatest wish is that you can feel the same level of security that I do.

Let me leave you with this story.

A few years after I started using this system, our incomes took unexpected hits at the same time our vehicle broke down. While saving up for a new car, we only had the food I had stored, and months went by without anyone realizing that. Why? Because nothing changed. I was already making most of our meals from my food storage, so when crunch time came, the only person who noticed that I was digging deeper into our food supply was me.

A quick review of everything we've learned:

I'M HAPPY FOR PEOPLE who like to buy MREs and food storage kits. My only concern is, have they ever eaten any of what they stored? When we're stressed out, it's a rough time to transition into new, strange food. What if you stored twenty years of MREs, and you find out that you can't stomach any of it? That's going to be a very rough time for everyone involved.

So please take the time to eat what you store. Before you invest hundreds of dollars into bulking up, eat them first and serve them as a regular meal. Eat it on and off for a month. You don't have to tell anyone what you're doing, just serve it as a new dish you're making. If after a month of this, your family still dislikes it, don't bulk up on it. Don't invest in food that you won't eat.

I don't care how long they last because it makes no difference if no one wants to eat it. In times of incredible stress, people long for what's familiar, and food is one of the best morale boosters. So in times of comfort and certainty, you can introduce new foods you wish to store long-term. Build up a taste for it when it's easy, and when it's hard, no one will notice.

I know how tempting it is to bulk up on a few food storage kits and forget about the whole thing. If you're going to do that, at least open one of them and serve it for a week. Because that's what it's going to be like when you need it. You won't be able to get new food, so you'll have to rely entirely on the food storage kits you bought. This will teach you what they taste like, how to prepare them, and how many of them your family will actually need. Because the box can say that one pack is one serving, but if you need to eat two to feel satisfied, then you have to consider doubling your supply. This is all information you won't gain until you pop open the box and get to eating.

And if you don't want to eat it now, what makes you think you'll want it more when you're panicking? If I'm hungry, I'll be sure to eat anything, right? Well, they found out during WW2 that people went hungry because they didn't want to eat the food they had stored. Yeah, you'll be able to choke it down a few times, but how many days will you be able to go on doing that? Slowly, day by day, you'll go longer and longer without eating.

This is not ideal for you or your family. Solve this problem by serving those MREs and see if they're worth storing. I'm not saying that those things taste bad and no one should ever store them. Please don't think that I'm badmouthing MREs or food storage kits; I'm simply stating that if you don't eat what you store, you won't know what you have until it's too late.

So the motto is eat what you store and store what you eat.

The second important thing to remember is that you eat your older supply first and store your new purchases. This means you will know where you're putting your purchases and when you bought them. Writing down the date on the items and the clipboard with a list of what you bought and when you bought it will greatly assist you in this matter.

I recommend that you keep your older supply on a shelf that is eye level while keeping the new purchases on a high shelf or floor level shelf. For the older supply, I put it on my eat shelf and for my new supply, I put it on my store shelf. By having the older supply at eye level, you make it easier to reach for when you're cooking, and you can easily avoid accidentally using your new purchases. Then when you go shopping, you move the items from the store shelf up to the eat shelf and restock the store shelf with what you just bought. Do it before you go shopping for a smoother experience.

The key to an efficient food storage plan is the knowledge that you gain from doing it. There are so many different variables at play with this. Temperature, moisture, light, time, food quality, and location all play different parts in this game of food preservation. If you're not paying attention to what's going bad and tweaking the storage conditions, you'll end up losing some food, but I promise you that it's nothing compared to how much you currently throw away.

By simply buying more non-perishables, the amount of food that goes into the trash will dramatically decrease.

If you want to seriously upgrade your food supply, learn how to preserve your veggies and meats by canning them. This takes more time and effort, of course. But remember that you trade that effort for money when you buy canned foods, and you trade time and effort for that money in the first place. So in a very real sense, everything will take time and effort, and where you put your focus is up to you. You can buy cheaper produce and meats, can them in batches, and save a nice chunk of money this route, so in a way that's like giving yourself a raise at work. Canning food is an art and will require you to learn new skills. It's not going to be a constant success when you're starting out and that's the price of learning.

Do you have a favorite crop that comes around once per year? For me, it's mango and lychee. When the season is going, there is an abundance of cheap fruits everywhere, and then once it's over, the prices shoot right back up. If I can preserve them when it's in season, I would be able to have them year-round at a reasonable price. Canning is not the only way to preserve things; I can also sun dry them or use a dehydrator. There is a much higher learning curve for drying food, so expect to lose more food during the learning phase. At least that has been my experience learning how to dry food in humid Hawaii. If you learn in a much drier location, sun drying might be a breeze.

• • • •

What might be stopping you from taking action?

YOUR WILLINGNESS TO learn and your willingness to change will affect every aspect of your life, not just food storage. Without both, no amount of information will affect your life. You're here reading this book because you want to benefit your life and your family. Don't ruin your efforts by being unwilling to change. By getting this far in the book, I can see that your willingness to learn is somewhat high but without the willingness to change, it will be for nothing.

Food is one of the hardest things to change because it's so closely tied to our childhood, our survival, and our culture. In a lot of ways, it's tied to our identity. Look at some of the chocolate lovers in your life and you can see how much of their identity is tied up in loving that one snack.

Because of this, we resist change in this area. It's hard to get people to change brands of potato chips, let alone anything else.

So if you learn how to paint and you don't paint, how has that information affected your life? It hasn't. You may have more art supplies, but your life has not experienced the power of painting. So unless you change the way you store your food, you have wasted all this time reading this book.

Before I tell you how to fix this, let us first learn how to gauge it because we all believe that we're flexible, but our actions may tell a different story. Pick your favorite activity in the world, whatever that may be, and ask yourself to apply this information, am I willing to give up that activity in exchange for this new activity? Am I willing to trade my favorite activity to work on this food system?

If you're not willing to give up any of the time you spend on that activity to apply this system, then your willingness to change is at zero. If you're willing to give it up for a week, it's at a 4, and if you're willing to go for a month, it's at a 6. If you're willing to commit a year to not doing your favorite activity to do these new actions, you, my friend, have a maxed out willingness to change at a 10.

So what if I'm at zero willingness to change? How do I increase my willingness to change? Have a clear powerful vision of what you want to do with the information. Imagine your family thriving and eating well when the rest of the world riots. I don't know about you, but during Covid, I realized how easy it was for the world to shut down with a few decisions.

While things are settling, your family will stay well-fed for months. This is the vision that I had for my family and what got me to change. A couple of lists and a simple storage system have completely freed me from all that anxiety. I didn't spend more on food; I spent the same amount monthly. I shifted the same funds into non-perishables and learned how to keep my food longer. Now I spend less because I'm wasting less. I don't have to keep refilling a supply of perishables; instead, I have a power-free pantry of non-perishables. It's simple but not easy.

Why is it not easy? Because it hurts to change my old habits. It took focus and willpower to stop buying way too many snacks and drinks. It hurts to grow sometimes; that's why they call it growing pains.

I wanted to run back to my old pattern of ignoring my food and how much food I was wasting. I didn't want to learn new skills or create ideal storage conditions. All of this resistance melted away in the light of my vision, and I was able to push through the growing pains, but it was not easy.

This system is simple but not easy, and if you can accept that, you'll be more prepared when you come face to face with the pain of overcoming automatic patterns. Splurging on fresh food, ignoring the guilt of our wasted ingredients, and not keeping track of our meals, are all old habits we'll need to change for us to take back the reins of our food supply. It's the way everyone else handles their food and you're going to have to step out of that flow. Do you ever wonder why so many people live paycheck to paycheck? Because their fridge is almost always stuffed with rotten food. There's no security in an empty pantry, the only thing you'll gain from that is a constant worry about when your next meal will come. They can't eat their paycheck so what they're actually referring to is the cost of living. Food makes up a large portion of our living expenses. Even if I was homeless, that is one cost of living we can't get rid of. Even knowing all this information, I was reckless with my food supplies and lost so much food in the process. Hours of work paid for that food and I refused to track my food, leaving it up to chance that I maybe brought the right amount of food for myself or I might have to leave to grab take-out for the night. Why? Because I thought it was stupid to care so much about food.

I had to let go of this belief and move towards my vision of being more prepared. A process called Be set Free Fast by Larry Nims helped me release my old beliefs towards my identity so that I faced less resistance when I put these new habits into use. I was able to push through my discomforts with the help of this one mental process and nothing has radically altered my journey as much as having this ability in my back pocket. The process helps you release the stored emotions behind our beliefs. I was obsessed once I resolved a huge family hurt in one treatment of the process. I used this process to clear most of the mental blockages I had on my creative potential so that I could pursue my career in writing. I used this process to repair my relationships with my family and partner. I used it to clear anything that blocked the path to the change I wanted in my life. So using this process, I was able to confront my tight ties to food and release the beliefs which made me waste and ignore my food.

List of the Beliefs I cleared for food:

This is the way my mom does it so I should do it like her.

I'm too lazy to do all the work it needs.

Food doesn't matter, there's always more.

It's silly to keep records of food purchases.

It doesn't matter what I buy to eat.

Storing food is a waste of time.

I'm not a prepper. I don't need to stockpile anything.

It's pointless to try to control my food supply.

It's out of my control if I have food or not.

I'll leave all that work up to the stores.

Once I resolved the emotions behind those beliefs, I found myself more capable and willing to apply the changes. My emotions made me avoid those tasks but once I resolved the feelings that come up with food, I was able to keep better track of my habits. I started small and worked my way up to a 6 months supply. If you want to read more about how I release my beliefs, visit my website https://releasebeliefs.wordpress.com/ and learn how I can help you learn this process.

Just get started, one step at a time

YOU CAN START BY TRACKING a single month's supply of one food item at the store. Write the date of purchase on the boxes. When it goes bad, write the date on a box. Transfer this information onto a list.

Look, you have successfully created a report on one item.

Write down the answers to these questions below the data you've collected.

- Did you make it last a whole month or did you use it all too quickly?
- If it went bad, what seems to be the cause?
- Where was it stored? Conditions?
- Is there a way to make the item last longer?

Now you've answered that, you learned quite a bit about that one ingredient. Repeat this a few more times and you will have a decent understanding of your food supply. If you will invest in non-perishables at least once a month, you'll have a fair amount of food that is made to last long, stacking up in your pantry after a few shopping trips.

- Make a good space for that abundance that is dry, clean, and pest-free.

- Eat the older supply first and store the new stuff.

- Keep a list of what you put in and another list for when you need to buy more.

- Store what you eat and eat what you store.

Build on the habit slowly and you'll get there before you know it.

It's simple but not easy, remember?

••••

I WANT YOU TO CLOSE your eyes and see a future where you're sitting in your pantry and staring at walls of food. Your children are laughing and running around carefree. You're holding a list of all the food you know you have. You release a long sigh of relief and know that even if you don't buy any more food, your family will eat well for months. The noisy news can sell their fear as loud as they want but you're not buying because you know that you got this. You're free from the food chain even if it's only for a year. A year is a long time when everyone else is losing their minds.

••••

I'M WISHING YOU THE best of luck in finding amazing deals to bulk up on and the strength to keep going when your past patterns come knocking. I hope you savor your food, your family, and your life.

About the Author

Aloha, this is Bach Ly, coming at you from the big island of Hawaii. I'm a full time mother, and a part time author, with my two daughters and my wonderful life partner, Steven Frame. Learning the Be Set Free Fast process in my early 20's had been a key point in changing my life. And I passionately believe that BSFF (shorthand) is a tool that can greatly benefit anyone who is struggling with applying change. So obsessed I was, I enrolled in a 6 week training course for becoming a practitioner of BSFF with Larry Nims, himself. Now I offer one on one sessions on how to release beliefs.

For more information: visit my website releasebeliefs.wordpress.com[1]

If you want to read more about my personal life, you'll find fun stories here:

Bach and Gratitude's adventure Blog[2]

• • • •

1. https://releasebeliefs.wordpress.com/
2. https://bachgratitudeadventure.wordpress.com/

YOU CAN BUY IT HERE[3]

3. https://a.co/d/cFEPXHf

www.ingramcontent.com/pod-product-compliance
Lightning Source LLC
LaVergne TN
LVHW010456160826
845677LV00012B/2513

* 9 7 9 8 2 3 0 3 7 6 3 7 8 *